THE ELECTORAL COLLEGE AND THE AMERICAN IDEA OF DEMOCRACY

THE ELECTORAL COLLEGE AND THE AMERICAN IDEA OF DEMOCRACY

Martin Diamond

American Enterprise Institute for Public Policy Research
Washington, D.C.

Martin Diamond is professor of government and holds the Thomas and Dorothy Leavey Chair on the Foundations of American Freedom at Georgetown University.

ISBN 0-8447-3262-1

Library of Congress Catalog Card No. 77-81901

AEI Studies 163

Second printing, December 1979
Third printing, October **1980**

Printed in the United States of America

Contents

The Electoral College and the American Idea of Democracy

In 1967, a distinguished commission of the American Bar Association recommended that the Electoral College be scrapped and replaced by a nationwide popular vote for the President, with provision for a runoff election between the top two candidates in the event no candidate received at least 40 percent of the popular vote. This recommendation was passed by the House in 1969, came close to passage in the Senate in 1970, and is now once again upon us. It is this proposal that has just been endorsed by President Carter and that is being pressed upon Congress under the leadership of Senator Bayh.

The theme of this attack upon the Electoral College is well summarized in a much-quoted sentence from the 1969 ABA Report: "*The electoral college method of electing a President of the United States is archaic, undemocratic, complex, ambiguous, indirect, and dangerous.*"[1] These six charges may seem a bit harsh on a system that has worked well for a very long time, but they do provide a convenient topical outline for a brief defense of the basic principles and procedures of the Electoral College.

AN "ARCHAIC" SYSTEM?

The word *archaic* evokes all those Herblock and other cartoons that portray the Electoral College (or any other feature of the Constitution that is being caricatured) as a deaf, decrepit, old fogey left over from the colonial era. This is the characteristic rhetoric and imagery

[1] *Electing the President: A Report of the Commission on Electoral College Reform* (Chicago: American Bar Association, 1967), p. 3.

of contemporary criticism of our now nearly two-centuries old Constitution. But we ought not (and perhaps lawyers, especially, ought not) acquiesce too readily in the prejudice that whatever is old is archaic, in the ABA's pejorative use of that word. On the contrary, it may be argued that the proper political prejudice, if we are to have one, ought to be in favor of the long-persisting, of the tried and true—that our first inclination in constitutional matters ought to be that old is good and older is better. We should remind ourselves of some Aristotelian wisdom reformulated by James Madison in *The Federalist*, Number 49, when he warned that tinkering with the Constitution would deprive the system of government of "that veneration which time bestows on everything, and without which perhaps the wisest and freest governments would not possess the requisite stability." [2]

In other words, a long-standing constitutional arrangement secures, by its very age, that habitual popular acceptance which is an indispensable ingredient in constitutional legitimacy, that is, in the power of a constitution to be accepted and lived under by free men and women. By this reasoning, we should preserve the Electoral College—barring truly serious harm actually experienced under it—simply on grounds of its nearly two-centuries long history of tranquil popular acceptance. We who have seen so many free constitutions fail because they proved to be mere parchment, unrooted in the hearts and habits of the people, should be responsive to Madison's understated warning; we should readily agree that it would not be a "superfluous advantage" even to the most perfectly devised constitution to have the people's habitual acceptance on its side.[3]

But it is not necessary, in defense of the Electoral College, to rely on such sober (but startling nowadays) reasoning as that of Madison, because the Electoral College happens not to be an archaic element of our constitutional system. Not only is it not at all archaic, but one might say that it is the very model of up-to-date constitutional flexibility. Perhaps no other feature of the Constitution has had a greater capacity for dynamic historical adaptiveness. The electors became nullities; presidential elections became dramatic national contests; the federal elements in the process became strengthened by the general-ticket practice (that is, winner-take-all); modern mass political parties developed; campaigning moved from rather rigid sectionalism to the complexities of a modern technological society—and all this occurred tranquilly and legitimately within the original constitutional framework (as modified by the Twelfth Amendment).

[2] *The Federalist Papers*, ed. C. Rossiter (New York: Mentor Books, 1961), p. 314.
[3] Ibid., p. 315.

The Electoral College thus has experienced an immense historical evolution. But the remarkable fact is that while it now operates in historically transformed ways, in ways not at all as the Framers intended, it nonetheless still operates largely to the ends that they intended. What more could one ask of a constitutional provision?

To appreciate why the original electoral provisions proved so adaptable, we have to recollect what the original intention was. To do that, we have first to get something out of our heads, namely, the widespread notion that the intention behind the Electoral College was undemocratic, that the main aim was to remove the election from the people and place it in the hands of wise, autonomous, detached electors who, without reference to the popular will, would choose the man they deemed best for the job. Indeed, that is what the "archaic" charge really comes down to.

What is truly odd about this view is that the Electoral College *never* functioned in the archaically undemocratic manner we assume had been intended. In the first two elections, every single elector followed the known popular preference and cast a ballot for Washington. In 1796, every single elector cast a basically mandated ballot for either Adams or Jefferson, the two recognized choices of the electorate. And from that time on, electors have functioned for all practical purposes as the mandated agents of popular choice. Now if the Framers were as smart as they are made out to be, how did it happen that their archaically "elitist" instrumentality was so soon, so wholly, perverted? The answer is simple: It was not. The Electoral College never was fundamentally intended to operate in an undemocratic way. Rather, it was from the start thoroughly compatible with the democratic development that immediately ensued.

The device of independent electors as a substitute for direct popular election was hit upon for three reasons, none of which supports the thesis that the intention was fundamentally undemocratic. First, and above all, the electors were not devised as an undemocratic substitute for the popular will, but rather as a nationalizing substitute for the state legislatures. In short, the Electoral College, like so much else in the Constitution, was the product of the give-and-take and the compromises between the large and the small states, or, more precisely, between the confederalists—those who sought to retain much of the Articles of Confederation—and those who advocated a large, primarily national, republic. It will be remembered that there was a great struggle at the Constitutional Convention over this issue, which was the matrix out of which many of the main constitutional provisions emerged. As they did regarding the House of Representatives and the Senate, the confederalists fought hard to have the President selected by the state legislatures or by some means that retained the primacy of the states as states. It was to fend off this confederalizing threat that the leading Framers, Madison, James Wilson, and Gouverneur Morris, hit upon the Electoral College device. As a matter of fact, their own first choice was for a straight national popular vote; Wilson introduced that idea, and Madison and Morris endorsed it.[4] But when the "states righters" vehemently rejected it, Wilson, Madison, and Morris settled on the device of popularly elected electors. The Electoral College, thus, in its genesis and inspiration was not an anti-democratic but an anti-states-rights device, a way of keeping the election from the state politicians and giving it to the people.[5]

Second, the system of electors also had to be devised because most of the delegates to the Convention feared, not democracy itself, but only that a straightforward national election was "impracticable" in a country as large as the United States, given the poor internal communications it then had.[6] Many reasonably feared that, in these circumstances, the people simply could not have the national information about available candidates to make any real choice, let alone an intelligent one. And small-state partisans feared that, given this lack of information, ordinary voters would vote for favorite sons, with the result that large-state candidates would always win the presidential pluralities.[7] How seriously concerned the Framers were with this "communications gap" is shown by the famous faulty mechanism in the original provisions (the one that made possible the Jefferson-Burr deadlock in 1801). Each elector was originally to cast two votes, but without specifying which was for President and which for Vice-President. The Constitution required that at least one of these two votes be for a non-home-state candidate, the intention being to force the people and their electors to cast at least one electoral vote for a

[4] See *The Records of the Federal Convention of 1787*, ed. Max Farrand (New Haven: Yale University Press, 1966), vol. 1, pp. 68-69, 80, and vol. 2, pp. 29-31, 56-57, and 111.

[5] The "confederalists" won a temporary and partial victory at the Convention when the express provision for popular election of the electors was barely defeated. (See *The Records of the Federal Convention of 1787*, vol. 2, p. 404.) The Constitution finally provided that electors be elected "in such manner" as the state legislatures might decide. During the first three elections, electors were typically chosen by the state legislatures. By 1824, in all but six of the then twenty-four states, electors were being popularly elected. Ever since 1832, popular election has been the universal rule with negligible exceptions.

[6] For example, see James Wilson's explanation of the electoral device to the Pennsylvania ratifying convention. (*The Records of the Federal Convention of 1787*, vol. 3, p. 167.)

[7] See remarks of Madison and Oliver Ellsworth (Ibid., vol. 2, p. 111).

truly "continental" figure. Clearly, then, what the Framers were seeking was not an undemocratic way to substitute elite electors for the popular will; rather, as they claimed, they were trying to find a practicable way to extract from the popular will a nonparochial choice for the President.

The third reason for the electoral scheme likewise had nothing to do with frustrating democracy, but rather with the wide variety of suffrage practices in the states. Madison dealt with this problem at the Constitutional Convention on July 19, 1787. While election by "the people was in his opinion the fittest in itself," there was a serious circumstantial difficulty. "The right of suffrage was much more diffusive in the Northern than the Southern states; and the latter could have no influence in the election on the score of the Negroes. The substitution of electors obviated this difficulty." [8] That is, the electoral system would take care of the discrepancies between state voting population and total population of the states until, as Madison hoped and expected, slavery would be eliminated and suffrage discrepancies gradually disappeared. Again the intention was to find the most practical means in the circumstances to secure a popular choice of the President.

These were the main reasons, then, why the leading Framers settled for the electoral system instead of a national popular election, and none may fairly be characterized as undemocratic. But it must be admitted that the electoral device would not occur to us nowadays as a way to solve these practical problems that the founding generation faced, because we insist on more unqualifiedly populistic political instruments than they did. All of the founding generation were far more prepared than we to accept devices and processes that, to use their terms, refined or filtered the popular will; and a few of the founders, Hamilton, for example, did vainly hope that the electors would exercise such a degree of autonomy in choosing the President, as would perhaps exceed any reasonable democratic standard. This is what makes it easy for us to believe that the Electoral College was conceived undemocratically, rather than as a legitimately democratic response in the circumstances. But any fair and full reading of the evidence demands the conclusion suggested here: the majority of the Convention, and especially the leading architects of the Constitution, conceived the Electoral College simply as the most practical means by which to secure a free, democratic choice of an independent and effective chief executive.

---

[8] Ibid., vol. 2, p. 57.

Thus the essential spirit of the Electoral College, like that of the Constitution in general, was fundamentally democratic from the outset. That is why its mechanisms were so readily adaptable to the immense democratic developments of the last two centuries, the while preserving on balance certain unique principles of the American idea of democracy. And that is why, in defending the Electoral College, we are not clinging to an archaic eighteenth century institution. Rather, we are defending an electoral system that, because of its dynamic adaptiveness to changing circumstances, remains the most valuable way for us to choose a President.

The ABA's "archaic" charge is in fact an indictment of the electors as undemocratic. In dealing with that indictment, then, we seem to have anticipated the ABA's express charge that the Electoral College is "undemocratic." However, the chief contemporary attack on the Electoral College has little to do with the autonomous elector or, as is said, the "faithless elector." The autonomous elector could be amended out of existence (and without doing violence to the constitutional intention of the Electoral College), but this would not lessen the contemporary hostility to it as undemocratic. It is to the main problem of democracy and the Electoral College that we may now turn. But we may do so, after this historical inquiry into the purpose of the electors, emancipated from the prejudice that regards the Electoral College as having originated in an archaic, undemocratic intention.

AN "UNDEMOCRATIC" SYSTEM?

The gravamen of the "undemocratic" indictment of the Electoral College rests on the possibility that, because votes are aggregated within the states by the general-ticket system, in which the winner takes all, a loser in the national popular vote may nonetheless become President by winning a majority of the electoral votes of the states. This is supposedly the "loaded pistol" to our heads, our quadrennial game of Russian roulette; indeed, no terms seem lurid enough to express the contemporary horror at this possibility. This is what shocks our modern democratic sensibilities and, once the issue is permitted to be stated in this way, it takes a very brave man or woman to defend the Electoral College. But, fortunately, courage is not required; it suffices to reformulate the issue and get it on its proper footing.

In fact, presidential elections are already just about as democratic as they can be. We already have one-man, one-vote—*but in the states.* Elections are as freely and democratically contested as elections can be—*but in the states.* Victory always goes democratically to the winner of the raw popular vote—*but in the states.* The label given to the proposed reform, "direct popular election," is a misnomer; the elections have already become as directly popular as they can be—*but in the states.* Despite all their democratic rhetoric, the reformers do not propose to make our presidential elections more directly democratic, they only propose to make them more directly *national,* by entirely removing the states from the electoral process. Democracy thus is not the question regarding the Electoral College, federalism is: should our presidential elections remain in part *federally* democratic, or should we make them completely *nationally* democratic?

Whatever we decide, then, democracy itself is not at stake in our decision, only the prudential question of how to channel and organize the popular will. That makes everything easier. When the question is only whether the federally democratic aspect of the Electoral College should be abandoned in order to prevent the remotely possible election of a President who had not won the national popular vote, it does not seem so hard to opt for retaining some federalism in this homogenizing, centralizing age. When federalism has already been weakened, perhaps inevitably in modern circumstances, why further weaken the federal elements in our political system by destroying the informal federal element that has historically evolved in our system of presidential elections? The crucial general-ticket system, adopted in the 1830s for reasons pertinent then, has become in our time a constitutionally unplanned but vital support for federalism. Also called the "unit rule" system, it provides that the state's entire electoral vote goes to the winner of the popular vote in the state. Resting entirely on the voluntary legislative action of each state, this informal historical development, combined with the formal constitutional provision, has generated a federal element in the Electoral College which sends a federalizing impulse throughout our whole political process. It makes the states as states dramatically and pervasively important in the whole presidential selection process, from the earliest strategies in the nominating campaign through the convention and final election. Defederalize the presidential election—which is what direct popular election boils down to—and a contrary nationalizing impulse will gradually work its way throughout the political process. The nominating process naturally takes its cues from the electing process; were the President to be elected in a single national election, the same cuing process would continue, but in reverse.[9]

It is hard to think of a worse time than the present, when so much already tends toward excessive centralization, to strike an unnecessary blow at the federal quality of our political order. The federal aspect of the electoral controversy has received inadequate attention; indeed, it is regarded by many as irrelevant to it. The argument has been that the President is the representative of "all the people" and, hence, that he should be elected by them in a wholly national way, unimpeded by the interposition of the states. Unfortunately, the prevailing conception of federalism encourages this erroneous view. We tend nowadays to have a narrowed conception of federalism, limiting it to the reserved powers of the states. But by focusing exclusively on the division of power between the states and the central government, we overlook an equally vital aspect of federalism, namely, the federal elements in the central government itself. The Senate (which, after all, helps make laws for all the people) is the most obvious example; it is organized on the federal principle of equal representation of each state. Even the House of Representatives has federal elements in its design and mode of operation. There is no reason, then, why the President, admittedly the representative of all of us, cannot represent us and hence be elected by us in a way corresponding to our compoundly federal and national character. The ABA Report, for example, begs the question when it says that "it seems most appropriate that the election of the nation's only two national officers be by national referendum." [10] They are our two *central* officers. But they are not our two *national* officers; under the Constitution, they are our two *partly federal, partly national* officers. Why should we wish to change them into our two *wholly* national officers?

Since democracy as such is not implicated in our choice—but only whether to choose our Presidents in a partly federally democratic or a wholly national democratic way—we are perfectly free prudentially to choose the partly federal rather than the wholly national

---

[9] Alexander Bickel wisely stressed the importance of the Electoral College to federalism in *Reform and Continuity: The Electoral College, the Convention, and the Party System* (New York: Harper Colophon Books, 1971). See also excellent discussions in Judith Best, *The Case against the Direct Election of the President: A Defense of the Electoral College* (Ithaca: Cornell University Press, 1975), pp. 119 ff and 133 ff; and in Wallace S. Sayre and Judith H. Parris, *Voting for President: The Electoral College in the American Political System* (Washington, D.C.: The Brookings Institution, 1970), pp. 51 ff.

[10] *Electing the President*, p. 37.

route. We need only strip away from the Electoral College reformers their democratic rhetorical dress in order to make the sensible choice with good conscience.

Our consciences will be further eased when we note that the abhorrence of the federal aspect of the Electoral College—which causes the potential discrepancy between electoral and popular votes—cannot logically be limited to the Electoral College. It rests upon premises that necessitate abhorrence of any and all *district* forms of election. What is complained about in the Electoral College is endemic to all districted electoral systems, whether composed of states, or congressional districts, or parliamentary constituencies. If population is not exactly evenly distributed in all the districts (and it never can be), both in sheer numbers and in their political predispositions, then the possibility cannot be removed that the winner of a majority of the districts may not also be the winner of the raw popular vote. Regarding the British Parliament and the American Congress, for example, this is not merely a speculative matter or something that has not happened since 1888 (when Cleveland narrowly won the popular vote but lost the electoral vote, and thus the presidency, to Harrison), as in the case of the American presidency. It has happened more often and far more recently in England, where popular-minority governments are as possible as popular-minority Presidents are here.[11] It is a source of wonder that Electoral College critics, who are often partisans of the parliamentary system, regard with equanimity in that system what they cannot abide in the American case. There the whole power of government, both legislative and executive, is at stake in an election, while here only the executive power is involved.

And not only can and does the national popular-vote/district-vote discrepancy occur in England, it can and does occur here regarding control of both the House and the Senate. Why is it not a loaded pistol to our democratic heads when control over our lawmaking bodies can fall, and has fallen, into the hands of the party that lost in the national popular vote?[12] Have we come to view control of the presidency as so much more important than control of the House or

[11] In February 1974, although the Conservatives led Labour in the popular vote by 1 percentage point, Labour won three seats more than the Conservatives and was thereby enabled to form the government. See *Britain at the Polls: The Parliamentary Elections of 1974*, ed. Howard R. Penniman (Washington, D.C.: The American Enterprise Institute for Public Policy Research, 1975), p. 243.

[12] Since 1900, control of the House has gone four times (1910, 1916, 1938, 1942) to the party that lost the national popular vote. And, counting only the seats contested in any given election, the party that lost the national popular vote won the majority of Senate seats four times (1914, 1918, 1922, 1940) since the passage of the Sixteenth (direct popular election) Amendment in 1913.

Senate that we regard the discrepancy with horror in the one case and practically ignore it in the other? Granting the differences between electing a single chief executive and a numerous legislature, still the logic of the attack on the Electoral College also impugns the districted basis of both houses of Congress. The Senate has in fact been attacked on just that basis. Not only are popular votes for the Senate federally aggregated on a state basis, but also each state has an equal number of seats despite population inequalities; therefore, a discrepancy between the national popular vote and control of the Senate is likely to occur more often and more grossly than in the case of the presidency. Now just as the President is the President of all of the people, so too does the Senate make law and policy for the whole people, as we have noted. But we accept the districted basis of the Senate despite its "undemocratic" potential, partly because of its nearly sacrosanct constitutional status, and also because we see the wisdom of departing, in this instance, from strict national majoritarianism.

The House has largely escaped the "undemocratic" charge (especially now, after major reapportionment) despite the fact that its districted basis likewise creates a potential discrepancy between winning a majority of seats and winning the national popular vote for Congress. By the populistic reasoning and rhetoric that attacks the Electoral College, the House also fails the standard of national majoritarianism. But we quite ungrudgingly see the wisdom in departing from that standard in order to secure the many advantages of local districting. To indicate only a few: First, there is democratic responsiveness to local needs, interests, and opinions in general. Americans have always believed that there is more to democracy itself than merely maximizing national majoritarianism; our idea of democracy includes responsiveness to *local* majorities as well. Further, because of our multiplicity of interests, ethnic groups, religions, and races, we have always believed in local democratic responsiveness to geographically based minorities whose interests may otherwise be utterly neglected; such minorities secure vigorous direct representation, for example, only because of the districted basis of the House of Representatives. The state-by-state responsiveness of the Electoral College is an equally legitimate form of districted, local democratic responsiveness. There is also the security to liberty that results from the districted decentralization of the political basis of the legislature; and we cherish also the multiplication of opportunities for voluntary political participation that likewise results from that districted decentralization. Finally, we cherish the guarantee that districting provides, that power in the legislature will be nationally distributed, rather than concentrated in regional majorities, as would be possible in a non-districted election of the House. In short, in the case of both the House and the Senate, we accept the risk (and the occasional reality) of the national popular-vote/district-vote discrepancy because the advantages to be gained are great and because the House and Senate remain nationally democratic enough to satisfy any reasonable standard of democracy.

This kind of complex reasoning is the hallmark of the American idea of democracy: a taking into account of local as well as national democratic considerations and, even more importantly, blending democratic considerations with all the other things that contribute to political well-being. What is so disturbing about the attack on the Electoral College is the way the reasoning and the rhetoric of the reformers depart from this traditional American posture toward democracy. They scant or simply ignore all the other considerations and put the presidential election process to the single test of national democratic numbers. In contrast, the fundamental premise of the traditional American idea of democracy is that democracy, like all other forms of government, cannot be the be-all and end-all, the political *summum bonum;* rather, the political system must be made democratic enough and then structured, channeled, and moderated, so that on a democratic basis *all* the democratic considerations (in addition to the purely numerical) and all the other vital political considerations can be attended to.

The issue regarding the Electoral College, then, is not democratic reform versus the retention of an undemocratic system but rather a matter of which kind of democratic reasoning is to prevail in presidential elections—the traditional American idea that channels and constrains democracy or a rival idea that wishes democracy to be its entirely untrammeled and undifferentiated national self.

One more point may usefully be made regarding the charge that the Electoral College is undemocratic. I have already argued that our presidential elections under the Electoral College are thoroughly democratic, albeit partly federally democratic, and that democracy may profitably be blended with the advantages of districting. But even on the basis of purely national democratic terms, the potential popular-vote/electoral-vote discrepancy of the Electoral College may be tolerated with good democratic conscience.

Not only has the discrepancy not occurred for nearly a century, but no one even suggests that it is ever likely to occur save by a very small margin. The margin in the last actual occurrence, in 1888, was of minute proportions; and the imaginary "near misses"—those horrendous hypotheticals—are always in the range of zero to one-tenth of 1 percent.[13] The great undemocratic threat of the Electoral College, then, is the possibility that, so to speak, of 80 million votes, 50 percent minus one would rule over 50 percent plus one. Now there really is something strange in escalating this popgun possibility into a loaded pistol. For one thing, the statistical margin of error in the vote count (let alone other kinds of errors and chance circumstances) is larger than any anticipated discrepancy; that is to say, the discrepancy might be only apparent and not real. But even granting the possibility that 50 percent minus one might prevail over 50 percent plus one, how undemocratic would that really be? The answer is suggested by the fact that, in the long history of democratic thought, the problem never even arose before the present, let alone troubled anyone. It took us to invent it. When we understand why, we will also see that it is a spurious problem or, at least, a trivial one.

Historically, the problem of democracy was not about minute margins of electoral victory, but about whether, say, 5 percent (the rich and wellborn few), should rule over 95 percent (the poor many), to use the classical terms. That is what the real struggles of democracy were all about. Only a severe case of doctrinaire myopia blinds us to that and makes us see, instead, a crisis in the mathematical niceties of elections where no fundamental democratic issues are involved. Democracy is not at stake in our elections, only the decision as to which shifting portion of an overall democratic electorate will temporarily capture executive office. What serious difference does it make to any fundamental democratic value if, in such elections, 50 percent minus one of the voters *might*—*very* infrequently—win the presidency from 50 percent plus one of the voters? Only a country as thoroughly and safely democratic as ours could invent the 50 percent problem and make a tempest in a democratic teapot out of it.

The irrelevance of the potential popular-vote/electoral-vote discrepancy to any important democratic value is illustrated if we consider the following question: Would the Electoral College reformers really regard it as a disaster for democracy if Franklin D. Roosevelt (or any liberal Democrat) had beaten Herbert Hoover (or any conservative Republican) in the electoral vote but had lost by a handful in the national popular vote? The question is not meant, of course, in any spirit of partisan twitting. Rather, it is intended to suggest that no

[13] For an astute discussion of the way such mathematical masochism "abstracts from political realities," see Judith Best, *The Case against Direct Election of the President*, pp. 78 ff.

sensible person could seriously regard it as a disaster for democracy if—to use the language of caricature—a coalition of the poor, of labor, of blacks, et al., had thus squeaked by a coalition of the rich, the powerful, the privileged, and the like. To point this out is not to depreciate the importance of such an electoral outcome for the course of public policy. It is only to deny that it would threaten or make a mockery of the democratic foundations of our political order. To think that it would is to ignore the relevant socioeconomic requisites of democracy, and to be panicked into wide-reaching constitutional revisions by the bogeyman of the 50 percent minus one possibility. To risk such revision for such a reason is to reduce democracy not only to a matter of mere numbers, but to minute numbers, and to abstract numbers, drained of all socioeconomic significance for democracy.[14]

A "COMPLEX" SYSTEM?

The ABA Report does not make clear what is "complex" about the Electoral College or why complexity as such is bad. Perhaps the fear is that voters are baffled by the complexity of the Electoral College and that their bafflement violates a democratic norm. It must be admitted that an opinion survey could easily be devised that shows the average voter to be shockingly ignorant of what the Electoral College is and how it operates. But, then, opinion surveys almost

[14] Not everything can be dealt with here, but a footnote excursion on one more staple charge against the Electoral College as undemocratic is irresistible. This concerns the alleged disenfranchisement of those who vote for the loser in each state; their votes are "wasted" because they drop out at the state level from further national calculations. Or even worse, as Senator Thomas Hart Benton long ago complained, popular votes for the loser are in effect added to those of the winner, because he gets the state's whole electoral vote. Those who are horrified by this may take some comfort in one interesting fact. Although such disenfranchisement does indeed occur in every state in every election, it has had absolutely no significance since 1888. A moment's reflection should make this clear. The disenfranchised who vote for the ultimate electoral winner in states where he loses have no complaint; their candidate wins anyway. But how about the disenfranchised who vote for the ultimate electoral loser in states where he loses? Would it make any difference if their votes, instead of dropping out of further calculation, were added to their candidates' national popular vote total, and if popular votes determined the election? The answer is obvious: only when their candidate, although the electoral vote loser, happens to be the popular vote winner. And that has not happened since 1888. Like the popular-vote/electoral-vote discrepancy, of which it is a rhetorically resonant echo, the disenfranchisement problem has been absolutely immaterial for nearly a century.

always show the average voter to be shockingly ignorant of whatever a survey happens to be asking him about. It all depends upon what kind of knowledge the voter is expected to have. I would argue that most voters have a solid working knowledge of what a presidential election is all about. They know that they are voting for the candidate of their choice and that the candidate with the most votes wins in their state. And when watching the results on television or reading about them in the papers, they surely discover how the election came out. However ignorant they may be of the details of the Electoral College, their ignorance does not seem to affect at all the intention and meaning of their vote, or their acceptance of the electoral outcome. What more is necessary than that? What is the use of making the process less complex?

However, the animus against the complexity of the Electoral College surely goes deeper than a fear that voters are unable to explain it when asked. There seems to be a hostility to complexity as such. This hostility has a long history. It goes back at least to those French Enlightenment thinkers who scolded John Adams for the unnecessary complexity, for example, of American bicameralism. However such complexity had helped to mitigate monarchical severities, of what possible use could bicameralism be, they asked, now that America had established popular government? When the people rule, they insisted, one branch is quite enough; no complexity should stand in the way of straightforwardly recording and carrying out the popular will. The answer to them, and to all like-minded democratic simplifiers ever since, derives from the very essence of American democracy, which is precisely to be complex. The American idea of democracy, as argued above, is to take into account both local and national considerations, and also to moderate democracy and blend it with as many other things as are necessary to the public good. That blending necessitates complexity.

The Electoral College is, of course, only one example of the complexity that characterizes our entire political system. Bicameralism is complex; federalism is complex; judicial review is complex; the suspensory executive veto is a complex arrangement; the Bill of Rights introduces a thousand complexities. Are these also to be faulted on grounds of complexity? If a kind of prissy intelligibility is to be made the standard for deciding what should remain and what should be simplified in American government, how much would be left in place? In all fairness, the question is not whether our political system or any part of it is complex, but whether there is a good reason for any particular complexity. The skeptical, self-doubting American idea of democracy does not assume that the rich complexity of democratic reality is exhausted by mere national majoritarianism, nor does it assume that all good things automatically flow from democracy. It therefore asks of any institution not only whether it is democratic, but also whether, while leaving the system democratic enough, it contributes to fulfilling the complex requirements of democracy and to securing some worthwhile purpose not secured simply by democracy itself. That is the only appropriate question regarding the complexity of the Electoral College.

Some of the affirmative answers to that question as regards our electoral institution—especially the federal element blended into our democracy by the historical development of the Electoral College—have already been suggested. Others will more conveniently come up under two of the remaining headings of the ABA Report's indictment against the Electoral College.[15] To these we may now proceed.

AN "AMBIGUOUS" SYSTEM?

This charge is rather puzzling. It is so far off the mark that a rebuttal is hardly required; rather, it supplies the opportunity to point out a particular advantage of the Electoral College in comparison with its proposed substitute. Far from speaking unclearly or confusingly, the Electoral College has delivered exceptionally prompt and unequivocal electoral pronouncements. This is not to say that there have never been any delays or uncertainties. Whenever an election is closely divided, as ours often have been and are likely to be, no election system can deliver prompt and absolutely certain verdicts, free of the ambiguity that inheres in the electorate's own behavior. But when a realistic rather than an utopian standard is applied, the Electoral College has to be rated an unqualified success. To deny this betrays a reluctance to credit the Electoral College with any merit at all. Or, perhaps, it is another instance of the human propensity, remarked on by Hobbes, to attribute all inconveniences to the particular form of government under which one lives, rather than to recognize that some inconveniences are intrinsic to government as such regardless of its

[15] One of the three remaining charges—that the Electoral College mode of electing the President is "indirect"—we may pass over. The ABA Report does not make much of the charge; and what it makes of it, we have already dealt with in discussing the status of the electors as originally intended and the federal mode of counting the presidential vote.

form.[16] This propensity seems to explain the finding of ambiguity in the way the present system works.

To judge fairly the charge of ambiguity, then, the Electoral College must be compared in this regard with other electoral systems and, especially, with the 40 percent plus/runoff system proposed by President Carter and Senator Bayh as its replacement. Under the proposed system, the nation forms a single electoral district; the candidate who gets the most popular votes wins, provided the winning total equals at least 40 percent of the total number of votes cast; failing that, there would be a runoff election between the two candidates who had the most votes. Let us consider the prospects for ambiguity under this proposed system, in comparison with the actual experience under the Electoral College.

The American electorate has a fundamental tendency to divide closely, with "photo finish" elections being almost the rule rather than the exception. The Electoral College almost always announces these close election outcomes with useful amplification. In purely numerical popular votes, an election outcome might be uncertain and vulnerable to challenge; but the Electoral College replaces the numerical uncertainty with an unambiguously visible constitutional majority that sustains the legitimacy of the electoral result. If this magnifying lens is removed, the "squeaker" aspect of our presidential elections will become more visible and, probably, much more troubling. For example, the problem of error and fraud, no doubt endemic in some degree to all electoral systems, could very well be aggravated under the proposed national system, because every single precinct polling place could come under bitter scrutiny as relevant to a close and disputed national outcome. In contrast, under the Electoral College, ambiguity of outcome sufficient even to warrant challenge is infrequent and is always limited to but a few states. Indeed, the massive and undeniable fact is that, for a whole century, the Electoral College has produced unambiguous outcomes in every single presidential election, accepted by the losing candidate and party and by the whole American people with unfaltering legitimacy.[17]

Not only is it extremely unlikely that the proposed replacement could match this record of unambiguity, but the 40 percent plus plurality provision could very well introduce a different and graver

[16] See Chapter 18 of Hobbes's *Leviathan* (Oxford: The Clarendon Press, 1909), p. 141.

[17] The last seriously disputed presidential result occurred after the Hayes-Tilden election of 1876. And even then, the dispute had nothing to do with any defects in the electoral system, but rather resulted from irrepressible conflicts in the tragic aftermath of the Civil War.

kind of ambiguity into our political system. This would not be uncertainty as to who is the winner, but a profounder uncertainty as to whether the winner is truly the choice of the American people. Under the modern Electoral College, we have elected popular-majority Presidents about half the time, and plurality Presidents with close to 50 percent of the vote the rest of the time, save for three who received less than 45 percent of the popular vote. This is a remarkable record of unambiguity in regard to public support compared with the history of most other democratic systems. But, given the dynamics of American political behavior, the proposed 40 percent plus plurality provision might very well *typically* produce winners at or just above the 40 percent level.

The Electoral College strongly encourages the two-party system by almost always narrowing the election to a race between the two major-party candidates. Obviously, when there are only two serious competitors, the winner usually has a majority or large plurality of the total vote cast. But, as we shall shortly see, the new system would encourage minor and maverick candidacies. This multiplication of competitors would likely reduce the winning margin to the bare 40 percent plurality requirement of the new system. If so, we would have traded in a majority- or high plurality-presidency for one in which nearly 60 percent of the people might often have voted against the incumbent. How ironic it would be if a reform demanded in the name of democracy and majority rule resulted in a permanent minority presidency!

A "DANGEROUS" SYSTEM?

"Dangers" of the Electoral College. It is not possible here to discuss all the dangers that alarm critics of the Electoral College, for example, the faithless electors, or a cabal of them,[18] or the problem of the contingency election in the House of Representatives. Some pose real enough problems and would have to be dealt with in a fuller discussion. But

[18] There have only been about ten of these (the exact number is in doubt) out of about twenty thousand electoral ballots casts—a tiny handful, hardly even a statistical trace. And never once has a "faithless" ballot been cast with the intention of influencing the outcome of an election. They have all been cast for symbolic purposes only, and, ironically enough, usually as a symbolic response to majority opinion in the aberrant elector's home constituency. In short, it is about as likely that "faithless electors" will usurp an election as it is that the English Crown will reassume the regal power of, say, Henry VIII. Neither likelihood seems great enough to warrant the constitutional transformation of either system.

the present remarks are limited to the main danger that the reformers fear, namely, the popular-vote/electoral-vote discrepancy. This is the loaded pistol pointed to our heads, the threat that necessitates radical constitutional revision. Now the funny thing about this loaded pistol is that the last time it went off, in 1888, no one got hurt; no one even hollered. As far as I can tell, there was hardly a ripple of constitutional discontent, not a trace of dangerous delegitimation, and nothing remotely resembling the crisis predicted by present-day critics of the Electoral College. But it must be sadly acknowledged that, the next time it happens, there might well be far greater public distress. It would be due, in large part, to the decades of populistic denunciation of the Electoral College; a kind of self-confirming prophecy would be at work.

All that is needed to defuse this danger is for the undermining of the moral authority of the Electoral College to cease. The American people will not, on their own initiative, react with rage if one of the near-misses actually occurs. As after 1888, they will go about their business and, perhaps, straighten things out in the next election, as when they elected Cleveland in 1892. They will go about their business as they did in a parallel instance, after Vice President Agnew's resignation and Watergate, when the provisions of the Twenty-fifth Amendment went doubly into effect. The democratic foundations of our political system, and even the vigor of the presidency, were not weakened by the temporary absence of the majority or plurality popular support that normally undergirds the presidency. There need be no dangerous weakening should the Electoral College again produce a temporary shortfall in popular support—if only the reformers cease to cry havoc, and if those who ought to speak up do so and help the American people learn to enjoy the compatibility of the Electoral College with the American idea of democracy.

Dangers of Direct Election. Not every danger alleged to inhere in our present electoral system could thus be made to evaporate merely by the exercise of our own common sense; like every political institution, the Electoral College contains dangerous possibilities. But this much may be said about them: all the dangers critics claim to see in the Electoral College are entirely matters of speculation. Some have never actually occurred, and others have not occurred for nearly a century. Nothing whatever has actually gone wrong with the Electoral College for a very long time. Experience has demonstrated that the dangers incident to the present system are neither grave nor likely to occur. But what of the dangers incident to the proposed reform? It is as important to speculate about them as to frighten ourselves with imaginary possibilities under the Electoral College. Three dangers seem seriously to threaten under the proposed reform: weakening the two-party system, weakening party politics generally, and further imperializing the presidency.

Many have warned that the 40 percent plus/runoff system would encourage minor parties and in time undermine the two-party system. The encouragement consists in the runoff provision of the proposed reform, that is, in the possibility that minor parties will get enough votes in the first election to force a runoff. Supporters of the proposed change deny this likelihood. For example, the ABA Report argues that a third party is unlikely to get the 20 percent of the popular vote necessary to force a runoff. Perhaps so, and this has been very reassuring to supporters of the reform. But why does it have to be just "a" third party? Why cannot the runoff be forced by the combined votes of a half dozen or more minor parties that enter the first election? Indeed, they are all there waiting in the wings. The most powerful single constraint on minor-party presidential candidacies has always been the "don't throw your vote away" fear that caused their support to melt as election day approached. Norman Thomas, who knew this better than anyone, was certain that a national popular election of the kind now proposed would have immensely improved the Socialist electoral results. Now this is not to say that the Electoral College alone is what prevents ideological parties like that of the Socialists from winning elections in America. Obviously, other and more powerful factors ultimately determine that. But what the electoral machinery can determine is whether such parties remain electorally irrelevant, minuscule failures, or whether they can achieve sufficient electoral success to fragment the present two-party system. The relevant question is not whether the proposed reform of the Electoral College would radically change the ideological complexion of American parties, but whether it would multiply their number.

Moreover, not only ideological parties would be encouraged by the proposed change, but also minor parties and minor candidacies of all sorts. Sectional third parties would not be weakened by the 40 percent plus/runoff arrangement; they would retain their sectional appeal and pick up additional votes all over the country. The threat that dissident wings might bolt from one of the two major parties would instantly become more credible and thereby more disruptive within them; sooner or later the habit of bolting would probably take hold. Would there not also be an inducement to militant wings of ethnic, racial, and religious groups to abandon the major party framework and go it alone? And, as the recent proliferation of primary candidacies suggests, would-be "charismatics" might frequently take their case to the general electorate, given the inducements of the proposed new machinery.[19]

All this might not happen immediately. The two-party habit is strong among us, and many factors would continue to give it strength. But the proposed reform of the Electoral College would remove or weaken what is generally regarded as the most powerful cause of the two-party system, namely, the presidency as a "single-member district." There would, of course, still be a single office finally to be won or lost, but *not in the first election.* That is the key. If runoffs become the rule, as is likely, the first election would become in effect a kind of two-member district. There would be two winners in it; we would have created a valuable new electoral prize—a second place finish in the preliminary election. This would be a boon to the strong minor candidacies; needing now only to seem a "viable" alternative for second place, they could more easily make a plausible case to potential supporters. But, more important, there would be something to win for nearly everyone in the first, or preliminary, election. Minor party votes now shrink away as the election nears and practically disappear on election day. As is well known, this is because minor-party supporters desert their preferred candidates to vote for the "lesser evil" of the major candidates. But the proposed reform would remove the reason to do so. On the contrary, as in multiparty parliamentary systems, the voter could vote with his heart because that would in fact also be the calculating thing to do. There would be plenty of time to vote for the lesser evil in the eventual runoff election. The trial heat would be the time to help the preferred minor party show its strength. Even a modest showing would enable the minor party to participate in the frenetic bargaining inevitably incident to runoff elections. And even a modest showing would establish a claim to the newly available public financing that would simultaneously be an inducement to run and a means to strengthen one's candidacy.

Let us examine an illustration of the difference under the two electoral systems. At present, opinion polls teach minor-party sup-

---

[19] See Nelson W. Polsby, *Political Promises* (New York: Oxford University Press, 1974), p. 161.

> The temptation under a direct election system would be strong for all manner of demagogues and statesmen—whoever can raise the money—to run, whether sectional candidates or movie idols with widely scattered following, to appeal directly to the people. So there would be a high probability that under the [direct election plan] . . . the run-off would be the true election, and the initial election would look a bit like the start of the Boston Marathon with its motley crowd of contestants.

porters to desert come election day; the voter sees that his party has no chance of winning and acts accordingly. Under the proposed system, the polls would give exactly the opposite signal: hold fast. The voter would see his party or candidate making a showing and would see that a runoff was guaranteed; he would have no reason to desert his party. The first election would, thus, cease to have the deterrent effect on minor parties; the prospect of the runoff would change everything. True, in such matters, prediction is difficult. But it is clearly likely that the two-party system would be dangerously weakened by the proposed reform, whereas it is certain that it has been created and strengthened under the Electoral College. Most Americans agree that the two-party system is a valuable way of channelling democracy because that mode of democratic decision produces valuable qualities of moderation, consensus, and stability. It follows then that the proposed reform threatens a serious injury to the American political system.

Not only might the change weaken the two-party system, but it might well also have an enfeebling effect on party politics generally. The regular party politicians, which is to say, the state and local politicians, would become less important to presidential candidates. This tendency is already evident in the effect the presidential primaries are having; regular party machinery is becoming less important in the nominating process, and the individual apparatus of the candidates more important. The defederalizing of the presidential election seems likely to strengthen this tendency. No longer needing to carry states, the presidential candidates would find the regular politicians, who are most valuable for tipping the balance in a state, of diminishing importance for their free-wheeling search for popular votes. They probably would rely more and more on direct-mail and media experts, and on purely personal coteries, in conducting campaigns that would rely primarily on the mass media. The consequence would seem to be to disengage the presidential campaign from the party machinery and from the states and to isolate the presidency from their moderating effect. If "merchandising" the President has become an increasingly dangerous tendency, nationalizing and plebiscitizing the presidency would seem calculated only to intensify the danger.

This raises, finally, the question of the effect of the proposed reform on the presidency as an institution, that is, on the "imperial presidency." The populistic rhetoric that denounces the Electoral College as undemocratic has had, since the time of the New Deal, a corollary inclination to inflate the importance of the presidency. In recent years, however, we have all learned to be cautious about the extent of presidential power. Yet the proposed change could only have an inflating effect on it. The presidency has always derived great moral authority and political power from the claim that the President is the only representative of all the people. Why increase the force of that claim by magnifying the national and plebiscitary foundations of the presidency? This would be to enhance the presidential claims at just the moment when so much fear had been expressed about the "imperial presidency."

* * *

Many who deal with the Electoral College are concerned chiefly with its consequences for partisan purposes. They support or oppose it because of its alleged tendency to push the presidency in a liberal direction. As for myself, I am not at all sure what those partisan effects used to be, are now, or will become in the future. Accordingly, it seems a good time to rise above party considerations to the level of constitutional principle. On that level, it seems quite clear to me that the effects of the proposed change are likely to be quite bad. And it likewise seems quite clear to me that the Electoral College is easy to defend, once one gets the hang of it. It is a paradigm of the American idea of democracy. Thus to defend it is not only to help retain a valuable part of our political system, but also to help rediscover what the American idea of democracy is.